S0-BJJ-025

THE BERKSHIRES

THE BERKSHIRES

Bill Binzen

THE GLOBE PEQUOT PRESS
Chester, Connecticut

© 1986 by Bill Binzen

All rights reserved. No part of this book may be reproduced or transmitted in any form by any means, electronic or mechanical, including photocopying and recording, or by any information storage and retrieval system, except as may be expressly permitted by the 1976 Copyright Act or by the publisher. Requests for permission should be made in writing to the Globe Pequot Press, 138 West Main Street, Chester, Connecticut 06412.

Design by Fortunato Agliagoro

Library of Congress Cataloging-in-Publication Data

Binzen, Bill
    The Berkshires/Bill Binzen.–1st ed.
        p.   cm.
    Reprint. Originally published: Toronto: Skyline Press. c1986.
    ISBN 0-87106-502-9
    1. Berkshire Hills (Mass.)–Description and travel–Views.
    I. Title.
    [F72.B5B69 1989]
    974.4 1–dc19   89-31211
                                                                           CIP

Printed in Hong Kong by Everbest Printing Co. Ltd.
First Edition/Second Printing

INTRODUCTION

When I opened my mail one day a few years ago and read a letter which suggested the possibility of my doing a book of photographs on the Berkshires, I couldn't have been more intrigued. The Berkshires are, after all, just down the road and they are among my favorite places in all the world—and certainly the place I know best and have the greatest feeling for. The prospect of meandering around the Berkshires over the course of a year, exploring the villages and country roads and seeing what the people are up to filled me with delight.

An encyclopedia would tell us that the Berkshires are a part of the Appalachian system and a continuation of the Green Mountains of Vermont. It is a rolling highland of long, wooded ridges fairly uniform in height, broken and intersected by valleys. With its numerous lakes and overall appearance, it is often compared with the English lake country.

The area known as the Berkshires includes Berkshire County—the westernmost county in Massachusetts. The Berkshires do not have a precise border that I know of, so I beg to be excused if I seem to have gone too far, or not far enough, in certain directions. To the north I stopped at the Vermont border and to the west at the New York line. While the countryside beyond these borders is very lovely indeed, each seems to me to have a personality of its own, somewhat removed from that of the Berkshires. To the east I followed a rather jagged line not actually drawn on a map but determined only by intuition. To the south I included the Litchfield Hills in the northwest corner of Connecticut, which are geographically part of the Berkshires.

There is a wonderful balance in the natural world of the Berkshires. The mountains are not too high but high enough; the valleys are not too deep but deep enough; the lakes are not too big but big enough. They all seem to work together in perfect harmony.

It's a fact that there are no big booming spectacles in the Berkshires—nothing absolutely bowls you over. Rather there is a succession of little things that attract your attention and make you feel enriched for having observed them. It may be the line of the hilltops above the trees, or the way a stream meanders through a meadow.

There can't be many places in the world where the flow of the seasons is as interesting and as rewarding to the eye as in the Berkshires. Each season has a distinct personality and each seems to relish expressing itself to the fullest.

Complementing the natural world, but equally as interesting, are sights that take us back to Colonial times; old stone fences, the village greens, the winding roads, the wonderful churches, the fields cleared out of the woods, the ancient gravestones—all are reminders of the past in a way that is both graphic and emotional.

But, of course, there is more to the Berkshires than scenery and history. There are the people today who farm the land, tend the shops, teach the children and do the thousand and one other things that occupy people nearly everywhere. Some of these folks have roots going back generations, some have just moved in, but most I've met seem to feel that they wouldn't ever want to live any place else and, after all, that's the way it should be!

BILL BINZEN

1 There are some who would say that, in its own quiet way, there is no place on earth more pleasant than the Berkshires.

2 There is much to suggest that those who came before us were very capable of creating beauty in their own right, as this church spire in Litchfield, Connecticut would suggest.

3 (*right*) The Berkshires are still very rural, as they were in days gone by. This corn field is in Ashley Falls, Massachusetts.

4 After a long Berkshire winter what could be more inviting than the spring flowers at the Berkshire Garden Center in Stockbridge, Massachusetts?

5 (*right*) From 1902–12 Edith Wharton lived at The Mount, the estate she built at Lenox, Massachusetts which is now open to visitors. Some of her best known novels, including *Ethan Frome*, were written during this period.

6 It's pretty hard to drive very far in the Berkshires without passing an
antique shop. This one is in Sheffield, Massachusetts.

7 (*right*) White horse and red barn in Sheffield.

8 Ever since 1928, the town band of Salisbury, Connecticut, seen here playing at the Town Grove, has been making some of the most rousing music one could hope to hear.

9 (*right*) Soccer players at the Hotchkiss School in Lakeville, Connecticut wait their chance for a bit of the action.

10 The Rising Paper Company on the bank of the Housatonic River in Housatonic, Massachusetts has been making fine paper at this spot since 1900.

11 (*right*) Looking down on Tyringham, Massachusetts from the west one can easily imagine that the scene hasn't changed much in a century or more.

12 (*left*) The colors of spring can be as subtle as the colors of autumn are flamboyant.

13 The Berkshires are well endowed with old graveyards such as this one in Sharon, Connecticut. Often their gravestones hark back to the earliest days of Colonial settlement.

14 The Church on the Hill in Lenox, Massachusetts looks down benevolently upon those heading north out of the village. This Congregational Church was built in 1805.

15 (*right*) This eye-catching Victorian house sits along a quiet side street in Hinsdale, Massachusetts.

16 What better way to spend a sunny afternoon in July than on the porch of the Red Lion Inn in Stockbridge, Massachusetts?

17 (right) A cool stroll on a warm summer's day under a row of linden trees in Stockbridge, Massachusetts.

18 (*left*) A Kent School crew in Kent, Connecticut about to take to the Housatonic River for a race on a Saturday in May.

19 Visiting Morris Dancers do some fancy stepping by the green in Ashley Falls, Massachusetts. They wear bells 'to ward off evil spirits.'

20 Throughout the Berkshires volunteer firemen perform invaluable service to their communities. Here a raw recruit takes the wheel.

21 (right) First Graders in South Egremont, Massachusetts await the arrival of a schoolbus to take them home.

22 Gloriosa daisies peek over the fence at passersby along a street in Lenox, Massachusetts.

23 (*right*) A serpentine line of waiting school buses suggests the winding country lanes along which children are driven to school in the Berkshires.

24 A Civil War statue catches the late afternoon sun as it gazes across North Adams, Massachusetts and towards the west.

25 The spire of the First Congregational Church in Lee, Massachusetts
rises over buildings along the main street.

26 The whole town turned out for the climax of Dalton, Massachusetts'
Bicentennial Week—a nostalgic parade on a beautiful day in June.

27 The Shed at Tanglewood in Lenox, Massachusetts is not the only place on the grounds where great music is heard. Here, an audience is enjoying an *al fresco* performance during *Tanglewood on Parade* late in August.

28 (*left*) If Grant Wood chanced to look down from above he might be amused by this scene at the Berkshire Garden Center's annual Harvest Festival.

29 When it comes to ivy-covered walls Williams College in Williamstown, Massachusetts can certainly compete with the best of them.

30 At Chesterwood in Stockbridge, Massachusetts one can visit the summer estate and studio of Daniel Chester French, the sculptor of *Seated Lincoln* in the Lincoln Memorial in Washington, D.C. Exhibits by contemporary sculptors are assembled every summer in the gardens at Chesterwood.

31 (*right*) A farm sits tranquilly on the rolling hills near Richmond, Massachusetts.

32 On certain days the clouds over the Berkshires seem determined to steal the scene from whatever lies below.

33 (*right*) A fine Victorian house resides in uncrowded splendor in Cheshire, Massachusetts.

34 The front door of the Lanesborough Episcopal Church in Lanesborough, Massachusetts seems at one with the falling snow.

35 (*right*) Snow resting on boughs and twigs makes a fine filigree along a road near Richmond, Massachusetts.

36 (left) The Berkshires without horses would be like strawberries without cream. This horse show is near Lenox, Massàchusetts.

37 A young apprentice helps to get ready the sets for a performance of *The Vinegar Tree* at the Berkshire Theater Festival in Stockbridge, Massachusetts.

38 (*left*) A simple arch seems to be extending an invitation into someone's secret garden.

39 A train pulls into the historic Canaan Union Station in Canaan, Connecticut. On weekends from May to November train buffs can enjoy a trip into the past along the banks of the Housatonic River as far south as Kent.

40 (*left*) The War of the Roses is fought again! Two members of The Society for Creative Anachronism are seen in hand-to-hand combat during 'The Battle of Bosworth' in a field near Sheffield, Massachusetts.

41 Young student dancers at Jacob's Pillow in Becket, Massachusetts carry their exuberance from practice in the studio straight into the out-of-doors.

42 A church in Otis, Massachusetts finds itself in the spotlight of the late afternoon sun.

43 (*right*) Pontoosuc Lake at Pittsfield, Massachusetts is a pleasant sight on a warm summer's day.

44 (*left*) Nothing suggests the arrival of summer more poetically than the blooming of the mountain laurel.

45 Life is still quiet and gracious among the handsome old houses of Litchfield, Connecticut.

46 (*left*) Winter doesn't like to be predictable. On occasion, it may come early and dust the foliage with powdered sugar.

47 A farm in the countryside above Great Barrington, Massachusetts patiently waits for spring.

48 In Housatonic, Massachusetts a wood sculptor works on a giant rocking horse of carved red oak. When completed it will represent eighteen months worth of work.

49 The Berkshires are generously endowed with artists and craftsmen. In Monterey, Massachusetts a potter goes about the work at hand.

IN

memory of

DEACON·NATHANIEL
BUELL.

who Departed this life the 27th
day of November: 1808.
in 75th year of
his age.

Lord I commit my Soul to thee
Accept the sacred trust.
Receive ...... ter part of me.
And w...... ......ous morning come.
Till deat...... ...... Saints shall rise

50 Veterans from battles of long ago are touchingly remembered in the graveyards of the Berkshires.

51 (right) On days like this it must be hard to concentrate on the books at Williams College in Williamstown, Massachusetts.

52 There's anticipation in the air just before the start of the annual
Memorial Day parade in Salisbury, Connecticut.

53 Young cyclists from France pause for a breather in the peaceful village
of Ashfield, Massachusetts.

54 (*left*) A farmer's work is never done. There is always one more cow to milk or a fence to mend.

55 These Black Angus cattle must be wondering where all that nice grass disappeared to overnight.

56 This hand-painted highway sign, standing at a strategic corner of the village green in Norfolk, Connecticut, has been pointing innumerable travellers to their destinations for some 140 years.

57 Spruced up Victorian houses along Church Street in North Adams,
Massachusetts face today with cheerful facades. At one point the wreck-
ing ball was just days away from demolishing them.

58 The course of a road race in Sheffield, Massachusetts takes runners through the oldest covered bridge in Massachusetts.

59 (right) It's tradition, at Brodie Mountain near New Ashford, Massachusetts, to have a festive end-of-the-season day of skiing on Saint Patrick's Day.

60 (*left*) Berkshire farmers of a few generations back would be somewhat alarmed to see their fields in autumn dotted with curious giant jellyrolls such as these.

61 Herman Melville bought this house in Pittsfield, Massachusetts in 1850. He named it 'Arrowhead' and it was here that he wrote *Moby Dick*. Today it is open to visitors.

62 (*left*) When it's 10 above zero and the wind is blowing one can only hope that there will be a cozy fire at the end of the road.

63 There is something quite moving about the first snow of winter. Here it is in Great Barrington, Massachusetts.

64 A Williams College student turns her back on Edgar Degas' *Little Dancer* to study a painting by Renoir at the Clark Art Institute in Williamstown, Massachusetts.

65 A young lad contemplates some of the delicious choices to be found within this bakery in Great Barrington, Massachusetts.

66 (*left*) Picnickers on the lawns of the Berkshire School in Sheffield, Massachusetts anticipate a summer performance of the Brahms *Requiem* by members of the Berkshire Choral Institute.

67 Many a rousing hockey game has taken place down through the years on Factory Pond in Lakeville, Connecticut.

68 In the country fetching the mail is a certain way of getting some fresh air. These mail boxes are awaiting their daily delivery in Falls Village, Connecticut.

69 (*right*) Wintry hedges serve as splendid ramparts for this Stockbridge, Massachusetts residence.

70 (*left*) On this hillside high above Lake Mahkeenac in Lenox, Massachusetts there once stood 'Shadowbrook', the most elegant mansion in all the Berkshires; but time and a disastrous fire swept all that away.

71 'Naumkeag', the many-gabled summer mansion designed by Stanford White in Stockbridge, Massachusetts was built in 1886 for Ambassador and Mrs Joseph Hodges Choate.

72 A lone Indian on the Mohawk Trail, west of Charlemont, Massachusetts, reflects on the changes time has wrought on his meandering pathway.

73 (*right*) On occasion, when you have to get there in a hurry, you can't do much better than the Mass. Pike which flows effortlessly across the Berkshires from east to west.

74 Citizens Hall at Interlaken is the home of the Lenox Arts Center.

75 (*right*) This cluster in Sharon, Connecticut refutes the notion that all Berkshire barns must be red.

76 One could do worse in the summertime than live in a white clapboard house surrounded by a garden of flowers. This scene is in South Williams-town, Massachusetts.

77 (*right*) A street in South Egremont, Massachusetts reflects a magic moment in early October when the leaves are at their most resplendent.

78 Every summer visitors enjoy the beautiful rose gardens and land-scaped grounds of 'Naumkeag' in Stockbridge, Massachusetts.

79 (*right*) The Hancock Shaker Village with its famous round barn is located a short distance west of Pittsfield, Massachusetts. It was first settled in 1780 but after the departure of the last two Shakers in 1960 it became a public museum.

80 Three small members of the Society of Brothers, a religious community in Norfolk, Connecticut, get a ride in their Father's wheelbarrow.

81 (*right*) Up, up, and away! Balloonists at a balloonfest on a farm near Cummington, Massachusetts prepare for an early dawn liftoff.

82 (*left*) A circus family at the Barrington Fair in Great Barrington, Massachusetts takes time out to polish up their act.

83 A spiral drive takes one to the top of Mount Greylock just west of Adams, Massachusetts. Here, some 3491 feet above sea level at the highest point in Massachusetts, one can enjoy an almost aerial view.

84 The covered bridge in West Cornwall, Connecticut was built of native oak. The men who built it could not have visualized in 1837 the outlandish vehicles that cross it today.

85 (*right*) These red silos in Southfield, Massachusetts have to sport fresh paint to compete with the autumn colors all around them.

86 (*left*) The canoe is as much a native of Berkshire lakes as the fish who swim in their sparkling waters.

87 Certain characters appear in the Berkshire countryside every year along about mid-October. This one popped up in West Cornwall, Connecticut.

88 Three cows, unaware of their importance to the economic well-being of the Berkshires, bask in the warmth of the late autumn sun.

89 (*right*) A solitary tree on the horizon appears as a lone actor on the Berkshire stage.

90 Some evenings, as the sun prepares to dip behind the Berkshire hills, there comes a stillness when man and nature are at one.